KETO COPYCAT RECIPES
- FOOD AND DRINKS -

Recreate your favorite recipes in the comfort of your own kitchen!
Boost your energy and stay in shape the ketogenic way!

JESSICA MEAL

TABLE OF CONTENTS

INTRODUCTION

The keto diet is an extremely popular dieting protocol that suggests a high fat and low or no-carb eating pattern. By increasing your intake of healthy fats and eliminating unnecessary carbs, sugars, and processed foods from your daily meals, you can improve your health. If weight loss is your priority, this diet will come in handy. By incorporating healthy and wholesome ingredients, consuming a moderate amount of protein, and no sugars, staying healthy and fit becomes easier. However, following this diet doesn't mean you need to compromise on your taste buds. Instead, it merely means you need to look for creative alternatives.

If you are already following the ketogenic diet, then please be prepared to be stunned. All the low-carb keto copycat recipes in this book will leave you feeling pleasantly surprised. These recipes will undoubtedly change how you view the regular keto diet menu. In fact, once you start cooking at home, chances are you will never want to go back to eating the unhealthy foods passed off as quality meals at restaurants.

In this book, you were given keto-friendly copycat recipes to recreate your favorite dishes from leading restaurants and fast-food chains. Whether it's Starbucks, Olive Garden, Popeye's, KFC, Taco Bell, Cinnabon, Cheesecake Factory, or any other, these recipes will cater to all your cravings. You no longer have to worry about compromising your diet for the sake of your taste buds. It's not just your taste buds, which will be left wanting more: your body will appreciate these keto-friendly meals as well. Tingle your taste buds and improve your health with the recipes given in this book. Dieting has never been this exciting, fun, or delicious. Get all the nutrients your body needs without piling up on the unnecessary carbs and sugars. Improve your health, achieve your fitness goals, and satiate your cravings with these keto-friendly copycat recipes.

All the recipes are extremely simple to follow, and they offer helpful tips and suggestions that can enhance their flavor profile. You can also customize your favorite recipes according to your tastes and preferences. Don't restrict yourself and allow your creativity to run wild while you experiment with these recipes.

Once you're armed with all the recipes given in this book, you get a chance to exercise control over the portions you consume, prevent the chances of overeating, cut down on your food bills, consume nutritious and good quality food, maintain hygiene and food safety, learn more about food, and reduce unhealthy ingredients. Apart from this, cooking is a great stress buster and helps engage all your senses. When you combine these benefits with the keto diet's benefits, it makes perfect sense to start cooking at home.

The key to achieving your fitness, health, and weight loss goals lies in your hands. The first step towards attaining these goals is shifting to the keto diet. With this book's help, you can achieve these goals while indulging in delicious and nutritious meals. So, take the first step today and get started with these recipes.

DESSERT

1. *Crème Brulee (Capital Grille)*

Preparation time: 10 minutes
Cooking time: 60 minutes
Servings: 12

Ingredients:

- 2 whole eggs
- 8 egg yolks
- 6 cups heavy cream
- 4 teaspoons vanilla bean paste
- 1/8 teaspoon salt
- 1 cup swerve confectioners'
- 6 tablespoons granular swerve or erythritol

Directions:

Place a heavy-bottomed pan on medium-high flame. Add cream and let it heat.

Once it starts bubbling, turn off the heat.

Whisk the yolks until light yellow in color. Add eggs and whisk well. Add swerve confectioners' and whisk until dissolved.

Add about a tablespoon of the cream mixture to the eggs and whisk constantly. Continue adding one tablespoon of the cream at a time and whisking, until all the cream is added. Strain with a wire mesh strainer and discard the vanilla seeds.

Pour mixture into 12 ramekins. Take a large baking dish. Pour enough boiling hot water to cover about 1 inch from the bottom of the dish.

Place the ramekins inside the baking dish. The water should be around ½ the height of the ramekins. Bake in batches if required.

Bake in a preheated oven at 300° F for about 45 minutes or until set. It may be slightly jiggly in the center but that is ok. It will be fine once chilled.

Remove from the oven and cool to room temperature. Chill for at least 2 hours.

To serve: sprinkle granular erythritol on top. Using a culinary torch, caramelize the top.

Serve either chilled or at room temperature.

Tip: If you do not have a culinary torch, broil for a couple of minutes until the top is brown. If you do not have vanilla paste, take 2 whole vanilla beans, scrape the seeds and use them. Add seeds to the cream while heating it. You can also use pure vanilla extract.

Nutrition: Calories 448 kcal, Fat 44 g, Total Carbohydrate 4 g, Net Carbohydrate 4 g, Fiber 0 g, Protein 3 g

2. Keto Snicker Bars (Snickers)

Preparation time: 10 minutes
Cooking time: 3: 4 minutes
Servings: 9

Ingredients:

For nougat layer

- ½ cup almond meal
- ¼ cup keto maple syrup
- 6 tablespoons coconut flour
- ¼ cup milk of your choice

For caramel layer

- ½ cup almond butter
- ½ cup coconut oil
- ½ cup sticky sweetener of your choice
- 2 tablespoons chopped nuts
- For chocolate coating:
- 1 cup sugar-free chocolate chips

Directions:

To make the nougat layer: grease a loaf pan with cooking spray. Line it with parchment paper before greasing.

Add coconut flour, almond meal and keto maple syrup into a bowl and mix well, then whisk in the milk.

Pour into the loaf pan. Chill for 20 minutes.

To make the caramel layer: mix almond butter, coconut oil and sweetener into a small saucepan. Place the saucepan over low heat and whisk until well incorporated. Add milk and whisk until smooth. Turn off the heat.

Spread the caramel over the nougat layer. Scatter nuts on top. Freeze for 15 minutes, then cut into 9 equal bars

Meanwhile, melt chocolate in a heatproof bowl, placed in a double boiler.

Dip each bar in the melted chocolate and place on a lined tray. Chill until chocolate has set, then serve.

Store leftovers in an airtight container in the refrigerator.

Tip: You can wrap individual bars in decorative cellophane sheets and give them as gifts.

Nutrition: 1 bar Calories 115 kcal, Fat 7 g, Total Carbohydrate 8 g, Net Carbohydrate 3 g, Fiber 5 g, Protein 4 g

3. Cupcakes (Hostess)

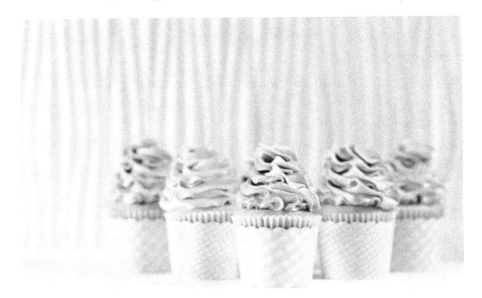

Preparation time: 40 minutes

Cooking time: 25 minutes

Servings: 30

Ingredients:

For cupcakes

- 4 cups almond flour
- 2/3 cup coconut flour
- 2 tablespoons instant coffee (optional)
- 1 teaspoon salt
- 1 ½ cups swerve sweetener
- 1 ½ cups unsweetened almond milk
- 1 1/3 cups dark cocoa
- 2 teaspoons vanilla extract
- 2/3 cup egg white protein powder

- 2 tablespoons baking powder
- 2/3 cup coconut oil
- 8 large eggs, at room temperature

For cream filling

- 2 cans (13.5 ounces each) full-fat coconut milk, chilled for 9: 10 hours
- 1 teaspoon vanilla extract
- 10 tablespoons powdered swerve sweetener, divided
- For chocolate ganache:
- 5 tablespoons coconut oil
- 6 tablespoons powdered swerve sweetener
- 4 ounces unsweetened dark chocolate
- 4 tablespoons cocoa powder

Directions:

To make the cake: line 2: 3 muffin pans (30 cups) with cupcake liners.

Add almond flour, coconut flour, cocoa powder, egg white powder, baking powder, salt and instant coffee into a mixing bowl and stir until well combined.

Add coconut oil and sweetener into a large mixing bowl and beat until well incorporated. Add eggs and vanilla extract and beat well.

Add about ¼ of the flour mixture and beat well. Continue adding flour mixture in batches.

Divide the batter into the prepared muffin cups. Fill them up to 2/3 of the cup.

Bake in a preheated oven 325° F for about 18: 22 minutes or until done.

Remove the muffin pans from the oven and let them cool for 10 minutes.

Remove the cakes from the pan and place on a wire rack to cool.

To make the cream filling: take the coconut milk out of the refrigerator just before making the filling. Place it upside-down on your countertop. Open the can, discard the liquid and use the coconut cream.

Add coconut cream into a large bowl. Stir in vanilla and 6 tablespoons sweetener and beat with an electric hand mixer until light and creamy.

Spoon the filling into a piping bag.

Turn all the cupcakes upside down and place them on a baking sheet. Take an icing nozzle and scoop out some of the cake from the center of each cupcake. Tap the nozzle to drop the scooped part. Retain the broadest part of the scooped cupcake and add the rest of it into another bowl. This part will work as a cover.

Pipe the filling into the cupcake holes. Retain some of the filling to decorate. Cover each cupcake with the retained part of the cupcake.

Now turn the cakes upside down again and place them on the baking sheet. Place the baking sheet in the refrigerator for a while.

To make chocolate ganache: add chocolate, coconut oil and sweetener into a pot. Place the pot over low flame. Stir frequently until the mixture melts and is well combined.

Turn off the heat and let it cool for 15: 20 minutes.

Spoon the ganache over each cupcake. Place it back in the refrigerator for some more time.

Add the remaining 4 tablespoons sweetener to the retained coconut cream mixture and stir well.

Spoon the mixture into an icing bag fitted with a thin nozzle. Pipe some design of your choice on top.

Serve.

Store leftovers into an airtight container and refrigerate until use. They can last for about a week.

Tip: Instead of discarding the coconut water from the coconut cans, use it in some other recipes, like smoothies, curry, or soups. The scooped cake can also be used in making other desserts as a garnish, or it can be served with whipped cream, fruit, or keto ice cream.

Nutrition: 1 cupcake

Calories 215 kcal, Fat 18.5 g, Total Carbohydrate 8.7 g, Net Carbohydrate 4.2 g, Fiber 4.5 g, Protein 6.7 g

4. *Very Cherry Ghirardelli Chocolate Cheesecake*

Preparation Time: 30 minutes
Cooking Time: 50 minutes
Servings: 14 Servings

Ingredients:

Crust

- ½ cup butter, melted
- 1 ½ cups chocolate cookies, crushed

Filling

¾ cup white sugar

1 cup dark chocolate chips, melted

1 cup heavy cream

1 tablespoon cornstarch

1 teaspoon vanilla extract

3 cups cream cheese

3 eggs

Topping

- 1 ¼ cups dark chocolate chips
- 1 cup heavy cream
- 1 cup Cherries
- ½ Ghirardelli Chocolate

Directions:

To make the crust, combine the ingredients in a container. Move the mixture to a 9-inch round cake pan coated with baking paper and press it thoroughly on the bottom of the pan.

To make the filling, combine the ingredients in a container until creamy. Pour the mixture over the crust , preheat your oven and bake at 330F for about fifty minutes.

Let cool down in the pan.

For the topping, bring the cream to a boil.

Turn off the heat and put in the chocolate. Stir until melted then let cool.

Top the cheesecake with the chilled topping chocolate cream, Ghirardelli chocolate and cherries.

This cheesecake tastes best chilled.

Nutrition: Calories 489 kcal, Fat 38.0g, Protein 7.4g, Carbohydrates 34.7g

5. *Tiramisu*

Preparation Time: 20 minutes
Cooking Time: 0 minutes
Servings: 2

Ingredients:

- ¼ cup heavy whipping cream
- 1 cup vanilla yogurt
- ½ cup fat-free milk
- ¼ cup brewed espresso, cooled
- 12 crisp ladyfinger biscuits
- 1 tablespoon cocoa powder
- Fresh raspberries, optional

Directions:

Take a mixing bowl and add the cream;

Use an electric handheld beater to beat the cream until it forms stiff peaks;

Stir in yogurt and mix gently with the cream until smooth;

Take an 8-inches square dish and spread half of the cream mixture at the bottom of the dish;

Take a shallow dish and add milk and espresso to this dish;

Mix these ingredients together and dip the 12 ladyfingers biscuits into the espresso mixture;

Leave the ladyfinger in the coffee. Once they are soaked, drain the excess liquid from the dish;

Spread the soft ladyfingers over the layer of the cream in the dish;

Add the remaining cream mixture over the ladyfinger biscuits;

Finally, sprinkle the cocoa power on top of the tiramisu and garnish with berries if desired;

Cover the tiramisu with a lid, or a plastic sheet then place the dish in the refrigerator;

Leave the cake in the refrigerator for 2 hours until well chilled;

Remove it from the refrigerator and slice it in squares;

Enjoy.

Nutrition: Calories 918 kcal, Protein 76.11 g, Fat 47.91 g, Carbohydrates 53.82 g

6. *Chocolate Chip Cookie Dough Cheesecake*

Preparation Time: 10 minutes
Cooking Time: 65 minutes
Servings: 2

Ingredients:
- 10 cream-filled chocolate sandwich cookies
- 1 tablespoon butter, melted
- 1 ½ packages (8 oz.) cream cheese, softened
- ½ cup of sugar
- ½ cup sour cream
- ⅛ cup all-purpose flour
- 1 teaspoon vanilla extract
- ⅛ teaspoon salt
- 1 ½ large eggs, room temperature, beaten

Directions:
Add the 10 cookies and butter to a food processor and hit the pulse button to crush the cookies;

Once the cookies and butter are thoroughly mixed, transfer the mixture to a bowl;

Take a 7-inches springform pan and grease it with cooking spray;

Keep ¾ cup of the cookies crumb mixture and spread the rest at the bottom of the springform and press it firmly;

Take another mixing bowl and add cream cheese and sugar;

Beat them together then add salt, vanilla, sour cream, and flour;

Continue beating the mixture and add eggs while mixing;

Once the eggs are well mixed in, fold in the reserved cookie crumbs and mix them well;

Spread this mixture into the crust evenly;

Set the oven's temperature to 325 degrees F for preheating;

Place the cheesecake pan in the oven and bake it for 65 minutes;

Once the cake is completely baked, remove it from the oven and allow it to cool at room temperature;

Remove the springform pan from the cake;

Place the cake in a platter with its crust side down;

Refrigerate the cake for 1 hour and then slice;

Serve.

Nutrition: Calories 388 kcal, Protein 5.38 g, Fat 17.87 g, Carbohydrates 52.38 g

7. *Fresh Strawberry Shortcake*

Preparation Time: 15 minutes

Cooking Time: 25 minutes

Servings: 2

Ingredients:

- ⅔ cup sugar
- ¼ cup shortening
- 1 large egg, room temperature
- 1 teaspoon vanilla extract
- ¼ teaspoon salt
- 1 ½ cups all-purpose flour
- 2 teaspoons baking powder
- ½ cup whole milk
- 1 cup heavy whipping cream, whipped
- 1 ½ quart fresh or frozen strawberries, sliced

Directions:

Take a mixing bowl and add shortening and sugar to this bowl;

Beat these ingredients together as you add vanilla and egg;

Mix salt, all-purpose flour, and baking powder in another bowl;

Add this dry mixture to the egg batter and mix well;

Stir in whole milk and mix well until it makes a smooth batter;

Take a 9-inches square baking pan and grease it with cooking spray;

Add the shortcake batter to the baking pan and spread it evenly;

Set the oven's temperature to exactly 350 degrees F for preheating;

Place the shortcake pan in the oven for 25 minutes approximately;

Once baked, insert a toothpick into the shortcake to check if it is completely baked;

Place the hot baked cake on a wire rack and leave it for 10 minutes to cool it down;

Run a cake knife around the edges of the cake, remove it from the pan and slice it into nine equal-sized squares;

Slice each square into half horizontally;

Add cream and strawberries in between the two layers of each cake square;

Make a sandwich with the two layers of the square and place them in the serving plates;

Garnish the shortcakes with desired toppings and serve.

Nutrition: Calories 497 kcal, Protein 7.04 g, Fat 26.45 g, Carbohydrates 57.54 g

8. *Upside Down Pineapple Cheesecake*

<u>Preparation Time</u>: 15 minutes
<u>Cooking Time:</u> 40 minutes
<u>Servings:</u> 2

Ingredients:
- ¾ cup packed brown sugar
- 4 slices canned pineapple
- 4 maraschino cherries

Filling
- 1 package (8 oz.) cream cheese, softened
- ½ cup confectioners' sugar
- 2 teaspoons all-purpose flour
- 1 teaspoon vanilla extract
- 1 large egg, room temperature, beaten
- ¼ cup crushed pineapple, well-drained

Directions:
Set the oven's temperature to exactly 350 degrees F for preheating;

Liberally grease an 8-inches baking pan with cooking spray;

Sprinkle brown sugar over the melted butter then place the pineapple slices over the sugar;

Place maraschino cherries at the center of each pineapple ring;

Transfer the pan to the refrigerator and leave it there until the filling is prepared;

Add flour, egg, vanilla extract, cream cheese and confectioners' sugar to a mixing bowl;

Beat these ingredients together with an electric beater until creamy and smooth. Then fold in a crushed pineapple;

Remove the pan from the refrigerator and pour in the cream cheese batter on top of the pineapple and cherry layer;

Set the oven's temperature to 325 degrees F for preheating;

Once preheated, place the cheesecake pan in the oven and bake it for 40 minutes;

When the cake is baked, remove the pan from the oven and place it over a wire rack; Leave the cake at room temperature for 10 minutes;

Run a cake knife around the edges of the cake and flip it over onto a large size plate; Remove the pan from the cake;

Cover the cake and refrigerate it for 1 hour; Slice and serve.

Nutrition: Calories 363 kcal, Protein 1.51 g, Fat 1.6 g, Carbohydrates 88.18 g

9. *Peanut Butter Cup Cheesecake*

<u>Preparation Time</u>: 25 minutes

<u>Cooking Time:</u> 66 minutes

<u>Servings</u>: 2

Ingredients:

- ⅔ cup graham cracker crumbs
- ⅛ cup sugar
- ⅛ cup Oreo cookie crumbs
- 3 tablespoons butter, melted
- ⅓ cup creamy peanut butter

Filling

- 1 ½ packages (8 oz.) cream cheese, softened
- ½ cup of sugar
- ½ cup sour cream
- ½ cup hot fudge ice cream topping
- ¾ teaspoon vanilla extract

- 2 small eggs, beaten
- 6 peanut butter cups, diced

Directions:

Take a large bowl and add sugar, butter, cracker and cookie crumbs to this bowl;

Mix these crust ingredients together until they form a coarse mixture;

Grease a 7 inches springform pan with cooking oil;

Add the crumbs mixture to the prepared pan and spread it evenly to make a crust;

Now transfer the baking pan to a baking sheet and place it in the oven;

Set the oven's temperature to exactly 350 degrees F for preheating;

Bake the prepared crust in the oven for 9 minutes at this temperature;

Once baked, allow the crust to cool on a wire rack;

Add peanut butter cups to a microwave-safe bowl and heat them for 30 seconds on high heat;

Spread the softened peanut butter on top of the baked crust;

Take a large-sized bowl and add sugar and cream cheese to this bowl;

Beat these ingredients together until smooth and creamy;

Stir in vanilla and sour cream and mix well;

Add eggs and continue beating on low speed for 5 minutes;

Keep 1 cup of this cream cheese mixture aside and spread the remaining mixture in the baked crust;

Add the fudge topping to a microwave-safe bowl and heat it for 30 seconds in the microwave;

Pour this melted topping into the reserved cream cheese mixture;

Mix well and pour over the white cream cheese filling in the pan. Use a toothpick to make swirling patterns on top;

Now return the baking pan to the oven and bake it for 65 minutes;

Once baked, place the pan on a wire rack to cool for 10 minutes;

Remove the cake from the pan;

Slice and serve.

Nutrition: Calories 1504 kcal, Protein 36.74 g, Fat 96.9 g, Carbohydrates 124.7 g

10.   *Cheesecake Factory Original*

<u>Preparation Time:</u> 20 minutes
<u>Cooking Time:</u> 60 minutes
<u>Servings:</u> 2-4

Ingredients:
Crust

- ⅔ cup graham cracker crumbs
- ⅛ teaspoon ground cinnamon
- 1/6 cup unsalted butter, melted

Filling

- 2 (8 oz.) packages cream cheese, softened
- ¾ cup sugar
- ¼ cup sour cream
- 1 teaspoon vanilla extract
- 3 small eggs

Topping

- ¼ cup sour cream
- 1 teaspoon sugar

Directions:
Set the oven's temperature to 475 degrees F for preheating;
Meanwhile, prepare the crust for the cake;
Add butter, cracker crumbs, and cinnamon to a food processor and blend them well to fine crumbs;
Take a 7-inches springform pan and layer it with parchment paper;
Spread the prepared crumbs mixture in the prepared pan and press it gently;
Place the crumbs crust in the freezer until the filling is ready;

Add sugar, cream cheese, vanilla, and sour cream to a mixing bowl;

Beat these ingredients together until creamy and smooth using an electric beater; Add eggs and continue beating the mixture until well mixed;

Remove the prepared cinnamon crust from the freezer and add the prepared filling to the crust;

Place the cheesecake pan in the preheated oven and bake it for 60 minutes;

Once baked, insert a toothpick into the cake to check if it's done;

Remove the cake from the oven and allow it to cool on a wire rack;

Meanwhile, prepare the topping by beating sour cream with sugar in a mixing bowl; Spread the cream topping over the cake and then refrigerate the cake for 4 hours; Slice and serve.

Nutrition: Calories 1028 kcal, Protein 21.7 g, Fat 77.01 g, Carbohydrates: 64.12 g

11. Strawberry Champagne Cheesecake

Preparation Time: 20 minutes
Cooking Time: 68 minutes
Servings: 2-4

Ingredients:

- 1 cup champagne
- 2 cups chocolate graham cracker crumbs
- 2 cups of sugar
- ½ cup butter, melted
- 1 cup fresh strawberries, sliced
- 3 packages (8 oz.) cream cheese, softened
- ½ cup sweetened condensed milk
- 2 tablespoons cornstarch
- 2 large eggs, beaten
- 2 large egg yolks

Topping
- 20 fresh strawberries, hulled
- ⅓ cup milk chocolate chips
- 1 teaspoon butter
- ⅓ cup white baking chips

Directions:

Add 1 cup champagne to a small-sized saucepan and place it over medium-high heat;

Cook the champagne to a boil then continue cooking for 8 minutes until it is reduced to ¼ cup;

Remove the champagne pan from the heat and allow it to cool;

Take a small-sized bowl and add butter, ½ cup sugar, and cracker crumbs;

Mix these crust ingredients together until they form a coarse mixture;

Take a 9-inches springform and grease it with cooking spray;

Spread the prepared crust in the pan and press it gently;

Arrange strawberry slices over the crust;

Take a large bowl and add remaining sugar and cream cheese;

Beat these ingredients together until smooth; then add cornstarch, reduced champagne, and condensed milk;

Whisk in egg yolks and eggs to the mixture while beating the mixture on low speed;

Pour this cream cheese mixture over the strawberry slices;

Spread the filling evenly with a spatula;

Set the oven's temperature to 325 degrees F;

Bake the cake for 60 minutes in the preheated oven;

After 60 minutes insert a toothpick to check if the cake is done;

Place the pan on the wire rack and allow it cool for 10 minutes;

Remove the cake from the pan and cover it to refrigerate for 1 hour;

Prepare the topping by melting chocolate chips with 1 teaspoon butter in a bowl in the microwave;

Arrange strawberries over the cake and drizzle the chocolate milk on top;

Lastly sprinkle white chocolate chips over the top to garnish;

Slice and serve.

Nutrition: Calories 659 kcal, Protein 6.83 g, Fat 35.68 g, Carbohydrates 70.22 g

12. Caramel Apple Cheesecake Bars

Preparation Time: 25 minutes
Cooking Time: 58 minutes
Servings: 2

Ingredients:

Crust

1 ½ cups crushed cinnamon graham crackers

- 6 tablespoons butter softened

Cheesecake

- 16 oz. cream cheese softened
- 2 large eggs
- ½ cup sour cream
- ½ cup granulated sugar
- 1 ½ teaspoons vanilla
- 1 ⅓ cups apple pie filling
- ⅓ cup caramel topping
- Streusel
- 4 tablespoons butter softened
- ½ cup packed brown sugar
- ⅓ cup walnuts
- ½ cup all-purpose flour
- 1 teaspoon cinnamon

Directions:

Take an 8-inches square pan and layer it with tin foil;

Add butter and graham crackers to the food processor and blend to a crumb consistency;

Set the oven's temperature to 350 degrees F;

Spread the crust mixture in the baking pan and bake this crust for 8 minutes;

Once baked, remove the baked crust from the oven and allow it to cool;

Add softened cream cheese to a steel mixing bowl and beat it for 1 minute;

Stir in sugar, vanilla, eggs, and sour cream;

Continue beating the sour cream mixture until it is creamy and smooth;

Spread ½ of this cream cheese filling in the baked crust;

Top this cream cheese layer with apple pie filling;

Add the remaining cream cheese filling on top and spread it evenly;

Drizzle caramel topping on top and make swirls with a toothpick;

Prepare streusel by mixing all its ingredients in a small bowl;

Spread the prepared streusel on top of the cheesecake;

Bake the cake for 50 minutes in the preheated oven;

Once baked, remove the cake from the oven and place it on a wire rack;

Allow the cake to cool and refrigerate for 4 hours;

Slice the cake into bar size portions and serve for two. Keep the remaining cheesecake bars in the refrigerator;

Enjoy.

Nutrition: Calories 1007 kcal, Protein 14.17 g, Fat 71.62 g, Carbohydrates: 81.53 g

13. Chocolate Tuxedo Cream Cheesecake Cake

Preparation Time: 30 minutes

Cooking Time: 46 minutes

Servings: 2-4

Ingredients:

Crust

- 2 cups crushed chocolate sandwich biscuits
- 4 tablespoons butter, melted
- Chocolate Cake
- ½ cup semi-sweet chocolate chips
- 4 tablespoons butter or margarine
- 6 tablespoons white sugar
- 2 eggs, beaten
- ¼ cup cocoa

Chocolate Cheesecake Layer

- 1 package (8 oz.) cream cheese, softened
- 6 tablespoons white sugar
- 3 tablespoons milk
- 1 egg, room temperature
- ¼ cup sour cream
- ¾ teaspoon vanilla extract
- 1 tablespoon flour
- 1 cup semi-sweet chocolate chips, melted

Mascarpone Cream Layer

- 1 ½ cups heavy cream
- ¼ cup confectioners' sugar
- 1 teaspoon vanilla extract
- 1 package (8 oz.) cream cheese, softened
- ¼ cup sour cream
- 1 cup white chocolate chips, melted
- ½ cup mini semi-sweet chocolate chips

Ganache Layer

- ½ cup heavy cream
- 1 cup semi-sweet chocolate chips

Directions:

Add chocolate biscuits along with melted butter to a food processor and pulse to crush the cookies;

Take a 9-inches springform pan and layer it with parchment paper then grease it with cooking spray;

Spread the crust mixture in the pan evenly and press it gently;

Add butter and chocolate chips to a microwave-safe bowl and heat for 30 seconds until the chocolate is melted;

Add sugar, egg and cocoa then then these ingredients well. Pour this mixture onto the crust.

Cream cheese filling

Add cream cheese and white sugar to a mixing bowl and beat it well until smooth and creamy;

Stir in egg and milk; then continue mixing the ingredients until fluffy;

Add flour, vanilla, and sour cream and mix well;

Fold in melted chocolate chips and mix gently until well combined;

Pour the cheesecake mixture onto the chocolate cake layer in the pan;

Set the oven's temperature to 350 degrees F;

Bake the cheesecake for 45 minutes in a preheated oven;

After 45 minutes insert a toothpick in the cake to check if it's done;

Place the pan on the wire rack and allow it to cool.

Mascarpone cream layer

Meanwhile, prepare the mascarpone cream layer;

Add cream, vanilla, and sugar to a mixing bowl and beat until it makes soft peaks;

Stir in cream cheese and beat until smooth and lump-free;

Add melted white chocolate and mix well;

Gently fold in mini chocolate chips and spread this topping over the cake;

Place the cake in the refrigerator for at least 4 hours;

Meanwhile prepare the chocolate ganache. Add chocolate chips and cream to a bowl;

Heat the two ingredients in the microwave for 30 seconds;

Mix well and pour it over the cake;

Refrigerate the cake again for 4 hours;

Slice and serve.

Nutrition: Calories 694 kcal, Protein 10.74 g, Fat 56.38 g, Carbohydrates: 40.14 g

14. Olive Garden White Chocolate Raspberry Cheesecake

Preparation Time: 45 minutes
Cooking Time: 1 hour 20 minutes
Servings: 12

Ingredients:

- 1 chocolate cookie crust
- 2 pounds cream cheese, softened
- ¾ cup sugar
- 2 teaspoons vanilla extract
- ½ teaspoon almond extract
- 4 large egg yolks
- ⅔ cup raspberry sauce
- ¼ pound white chocolate
- 2 cups whipped cream
- Cooking spray

Directions:

Line the outer 9-inch springform pan with aluminum foil. Spray the inside with a cooking spray, then add the crust of the cookie.

Preheat the oven to 325°F.

In a mixing bowl, combine the softened cream cheese, sugar, vanilla extract and almond extract using an electric mixer.

Add the egg yolks to the mixture. Mix until creamy and smooth.

Pour half of the batter into the crust. Place about ⅓ cup of raspberry sauce on top. Swirl with a table knife.

Pour the rest of the batter on top. Add another ⅓ cup of raspberry sauce and swirl again.

Fill a roasting pan with approximately 1 inch of water. Inside, place the springform pan. Bake for 1 hour and 20 minutes or until the cheesecake is fully cooked.

Turn off the oven but leave the pan inside with the door slightly open. Let cool for about 30–45 minutes. (This avoids cracks in the cheesecake.)

Remove the cheesecake from the oven and let cool to room temperature.

Cover & place in the refrigerator to chill overnight.

Decorate the cheesecake with shaved white chocolate and whipped cream. Slice and serve.

Nutrition: Calories 5937 Cal, Fat 448.11 g, Carbs 389.1 g, Fiber 8.8 g Sugar 311.63 g, Protein 106.69 g

15. Olive Garden Tiramisu

Preparation Time: 30 minutes
Cooking Time: 20 minutes
Servings: 8-10

Ingredients:
- ¼ cup whole milk
- ¾ cup granulated sugar
- 3 cups mascarpone cheese
- ½ pound cream cheese
- ¼ teaspoon vanilla extract
- 20–24 ladyfinger cookies
- ¼ cup cold espresso
- ¼ cup Kahlua coffee liqueur

- 2 teaspoons cocoa powder

Directions:

Boil in a medium saucepan over medium-high heat. Reduce heat and bring to a simmer.

In a medium bowl, whisk together the milk, sugar and two egg yolks. Place in the saucepan (or you can use a double broiler). Stir frequently for 10 minutes or until the sugar dissolves. Remove from heat and cool.

In a large bowl, combine the mascarpone, cream cheese and vanilla with an electric mixer. Mix until creamy. Add remaining egg yolk. Stir again.

In a small bowl, combine the espresso and Kahlua. Quickly dip each ladyfinger into the mixture, making sure it does not soak up too much liquid.

Place the ladyfingers side by side at the bottom of an 8×8 baking pan. Spoon half of the cheese mixture over the ladyfingers. Place more ladyfingers on top. Pour the remaining cheese mixture on top.

Using a strainer, dust cocoa powder on top of the last cheese mixture layer. Cover and chill for several hours. Slice and serve.

Nutrition: Calories 3313 Cal, Fat 207.26 g, Carbs 227.91 g, Fiber 3.3 g, Sugar 147.17 g, Protein 24 g, 3 egg yolks, divided

16. Olive Garden Lemon Cream Cake

Preparation Time: 45 minutes
Cooking Time: 45 – 60 minutes
Servings: 8-12

Ingredients:
Cake

- 1 cup cake flour
- 1¼ cups sugar, divided
- 1 cup egg whites (about 8 egg whites)
- 1 teaspoon cream of tartar
- ½ teaspoon salt
- 1 teaspoon vanilla
- 2 tablespoons powdered sugar, for dusting
- Crumb topping (optional)
- 2 cups all-purpose flour
- 5 teaspoons granulated sugar
- ½ teaspoon salt
- ½ cup (1 stick) butter, melted
- 1 teaspoon lemon juice
- 3 teaspoons water

Lemon cream filling

- 1 cup heavy cream
- 1 (8-ounce) package cream cheese
- 2½ cups powdered sugar
- 3 tablespoons lemon juice

Directions:

Preheat oven to 350°F.

Prepare the cake. Combine the flour and ¼ cup sugar and sift 4 times. To a grease-free mixing bowl, add egg whites, cream of tartar and salt. Using a whisk attachment, beat until frothy. While beating, add the remaining sugar gradually until mixture is fine-textured, with soft peaks. Add vanilla and fold in flour mixture, about ¼ cup at a time. Pour evenly into an ungreased 9-inch tube pan. Run a spatula through the batter to break up large air bubbles. Bake until a toothpick inserted at the center comes out clean (about 45–60 minutes). Invert to pan and let cool completely. Use a serrated knife to cut into 2 or 3 layers. Keep chilled until ready to be assembled.

To make the crumb topping (if using), preheat oven to 350°F and line a baking sheet. In a mixer bowl, combine the flour, sugar, and salt. Beat to blend. Add the melted butter, lemon juice, and water and beat until well-blended. Add more water by the teaspoon if the mixture looks like sand. The mixture is expected to form pea-sized clusters. Keep the sizes even for baking and texture. Spread in an even layer on a baking sheet and cook until golden brown (about 15 minutes). Let's just cool. If the cooked clusters are too large and difficult to break with the back of a spoon, use a blender or a food processor.

To make the cream filling, with an electric mixer, whip the cream until soft peaks form. In another bowl, beat the cream cheese, sugar and lemon juice until smooth. Gently fold into the whipped cream until well-blended. Refrigerate for at least 30 minutes.

To assemble the cake, Frost bottom layer with filling (½ of mixture for 2 layers or ⅓ for 3 layers). Repeat for second layer (if using 3 layers). Top with the last cake layer. Keep chilled.

Just before serving, add the powdered sugar and sprinkle with the crumb, topping, if desired.

Nutrition: Calories 2499 Cal, Fat 217.21 g, Carbs 1025.96 g, Fiber 644.39 g, Sugar 6 g, Protein 109.81 g

17. Olive Garden Chocolate Brownie Lasagna

Preparation Time: 15 minutes
Cooking Time: 60 minutes
Servings: 8

Ingredients:

- 6 cups cake flour, sifted
- 5¼ cups sugar
- 2¼ cups Hershey's cocoa
- 2 tablespoons baking soda
- 4½ cups milk
- 1½ cups butter
- 1 dozen large eggs
- 1 tablespoon vanilla extract
- 2 cups semi-sweet chocolate chips
- Butter cream

- ⅔ cup water
- ¼ cup meringue powder
- 12 cups confectioners' sugar, sifted
- 1¼ cups shortening
- ¾ teaspoon salt
- 1 teaspoon clear almond extract
- 1 teaspoon clear vanilla extract
- 1 teaspoon colorless butter flavor

Directions:

Preheat the oven to 350 Fahrenheit to make the cake. Grease 3 10-inch springform pans with a cooking spray.

Stir the sifted cake flour, sugar, cocoa, and baking soda into a mixing bowl. Add the butter and combine. Add the eggs, vanilla, and milk. Mix thoroughly.

Transfer to the pans for about 5 cups of cake batter. Bake for 40–50 minutes or until the toothpick is clean. Cool for 10 minutes before the pans are removed.

Make the butter cream by using an electric mixer to whip the water and meringue powder at high speed until peaks form.

Slowly add 4 cups of sugar. Beat at low speed. Add the shortening and then the remainder of the sugar. Add the salt and flavorings and continue to beat at low speed until smooth.

Thin out half of the frosting with some water. (This will be used to fill layers between the cakes.)

Assemble by placing one cake on a platter. Spread thinned frosting on top. Sprinkle with some semi-sweet chocolate chips, then top with the second layer of cake. Frost the top of the second layer with the thinned frosting. Place the third layer of cake on top. Frost the top with the remaining buttercream and sprinkle with more chocolate chips.

Cut into wedges and serve.

Nutrition: Calories 879 Cal, Fat 623.23 g, Carbs 3141.7 g, Fiber 65 g, Sugar 2446.11 g, Protein 190.49 g

18. Olive Garden S'mores Layer Cake

Preparation Time: 45 minutes
Cooking Time: 8-10 min
Chill Time: 8-12 hours
Servings: 10

Ingredients:
- Graham cracker layer
- 3 cups graham cracker crumbs
- 1 cup butter, melted
- Chocolate fudge layer
- 3 cups chocolate chips
- 2½ cups condensed milk

Marshmallow layer
- 3 packets gelatin
- ¾ cup warm water
- 3 7-ounce containers marshmallow fluff
- Chocolate ganache
- ¾ cup heavy cream
- 1 cup chocolate chips

Garnish
- Marshmallow fluff
- Mini-marshmallows
- Graham cracker crumbs & chunks
- Chocolate chunks

Directions:
The simplest way to ensure this cake comes out of the pan nicely is to line your springform pan with parchment at both the bottom and the sides. Then spray with nonstick cooking spray.

Mix the graham cracker crumbs and melted butter together in a mixing bowl. Press about ⅓ of the mixture into the bottom of the pan.

In a separate bowl, combine the chocolate chips and condensed milk. Microwave at 2-minute intervals until the chocolate melts. Stir until smooth.

Pour ⅓ of this mixture over the top of the graham cracker crumbs in the springform pan.

Dissolve 1 packet of gelatin in ¼ cup of warm water. When completely dissolved, mix the gelatin together with one jar of marshmallow fluff and stir until smooth. Spread the marshmallow mixture evenly over the top of the crumbs and chocolate in the springform pan.

Place the pan in the refrigerator for 5–10 minutes to set. Then remove from the refrigerator and repeat the layers: crumbs, chocolate and another packet of gelatin mixed with fluff. You will make 3 layers in total, refrigerating in between to ensure the layers remain separate.

Refrigerate overnight.

Before you are ready to serve, make the chocolate ganache by heating the heavy cream in the microwave for 3 minutes or until it starts to simmer lightly. Then pour it over the chocolate chips in a bowl. Stir until smooth, then let cool to room temperature.

Take the cake out of the refrigerator, remove the parchment paper and place it on a serving dish. Add the chocolate to the cake. It's all right if it drips down the sides; it adds flavor on its way down. Top with marshmallow fluff, toasted graham and chocolate chunks. Serve it.

Nutrition: Calories 1460 Cal, Fat 856.15 g, Carbs 920.06 g, Fiber 34.9 g, Sugar 685.29 g, Protein 57.26 g

19. Olive Garden Zeppoli

<u>Preparation Time</u>: 20 minutes

<u>Cooking Time:</u> 15 minutes

<u>Resting Time:</u> 90 minutes

<u>Servings:</u> 12

Ingredients:

- 1 (¼-ounce) package active dry yeast
- 1 cup water (divided)
- 1½ cups all-purpose flour
- 1 quart vegetable oil (for frying)
- 2 tablespoons confectioners' sugar
- Chocolate sauce for dipping

Directions:

In a saucepan, heat oil to 375°F.

Let the yeast dissolve in ½ cup of warm water for 10 minutes. Stir the remaining water into the bowl.

Add the flour and combine until a dough forms.

Knead on a smooth surface, then place into a greased bowl. Turn to coat the dough. Place a damp cloth on top to cover.

Let the dough rise for 1–1½ hours in a warm room. Cut and roll into golf-ball-sized pieces.

Fry until golden brown. Drain on top of a paper towel. Sprinkle with confectioners' sugar. Serve with

Nutrition: Calories 745 Cal, Fat 1.84 g, Carbs 159.04 g, Fiber 5.1 g, Sugar 16.16 g, Protein 19.37 g

20.   *Olive Garden Berry Crostata*

<u>Preparation Time:</u> 30 minutes plus 1 – 2 hours refrigeration
<u>Cooking Time:</u> 20 minutes
<u>Servings:</u> 2

Ingredients:
Crust
- 2 cups all-purpose flour
- ¼ cup granulated sugar
- ¾ teaspoon salt
- 1 cup (2 sticks) unsalted butter, chilled and diced
- 6 tablespoons ice-cold water

Filling
- 2 cups mixed berries of choice (like blackberries, raspberries and blueberries)
- 1 tablespoon granulated sugar
- ½ teaspoon cinnamon (optional)
- 1 tablespoon butter, diced
- Egg Wash
- 1 egg
- 1 tablespoon water
- Raspberry Sauce
- 2¾ cups (about 12 ounces) fresh raspberries
- 1 tablespoon sugar, or according to taste
- 1 teaspoon vanilla
- 1 tablespoon brandy (optional)

Toppings
- 2 scoops vanilla ice cream
- Raspberry syrup, for drizzling (recipe above)

Directions:

Just make the crust. Add flour, sugar and salt to your food processor. Pulse a couple of times to mix. Add the butter and pulse until the mixture is like a corn meal. Add the water to the stream while mixing until the mixture holds together. There's got to be some pea-sized butter pieces. Divide the dough into 2 balls, flatten it into thick disks and cover with plastic wrap. Chill for at least 1 hour of the night.

Prepare the filling. Toss berries in sugar and cinnamon (if using). Keep butter cold, to be added eventually.

Prepare the egg wash. Whisk the egg and water together in a small bowl.

Prepare the raspberry sauce. Mix the ingredients using a food processor or blender. Cover and refrigerate until ready to use.

Assemble the crostata.

Preheat oven to 350°F and line a baking sheet.

Roll out the dough into two 11-inch circles.

Place a cup of filling at the center of each, leaving about a 2-inch edge.

Fold and flute the edge over the filling, leaving some of it exposed at the center.

Place on lined baking sheet.

Brush with egg wash.

Sprinkle filling with reserved butter.

Bake until crust is golden brown (about 20 minutes).

Serve with scoops of ice cream, drizzled with raspberry sauce.

Nutrition: Calories 640 Cal, Fat 29 g, Carbs 47 g, Fiber 8 g, Sugar 210.06 g, Protein 7 g, Sodium 350 mg

21. Olive Garden Black Tie Mousse Cake

Preparation Time: 3 hours

Cooking Time: 35 minutes

Servings: 8-10

Ingredients:

Bottom Layer

- 1 (18 ounces) package of ordinary cake mix (devil's food)

Second Layer

- 1 teaspoon of unflavored gelatin
- 1 tablespoon of cold water
- 2 teaspoons of boiling water

- 4 ounces of semi-sweet chocolate chips
- 4 ounces of cream cheese,
- 3⁄4 cup heavy cream
- 1⁄2 teaspoon of granulated sugar

Third Layer

- 3 egg yolks
- 1⁄4 cup of granulated sugar 3
- 3 tablespoons flour
- 1 teaspoon Knox unflavored gelatin
- 1 3⁄4 cups heavy cream
- 1 teaspoon vanilla extract

Fourth Layer

- 1 1⁄2 cups heavy cream
- 2 tablespoons butter
- 18 ounces semi-sweet chocolate chips
- 1⁄2 cup white chocolate chips (optional)

Directions:

You will have to make four layers.

First Layer (Bottom layer)

Bake using 2 round panes according to the directions on the box, then cool. Using the cake from one pan as one layer until cooled (you don't need the second cake from the second pan, that is, you only need half the cake recipe from the box). Place this round cake underneath a cheesecake box. Press and flatten the cake a little with your fingertips. This is the four-legged bottom layer.

Second Layer (Chocolate Mousse)

Mix the chocolate and the cream cheese. Let's let it cool. Soften the gelatin for 1 minute with cold water, then add the boiling water, mix until dissolved and clear. Let this cool while the heavy cream and sugar are whipped in. Remove gelatin as the cream starts to thicken. Keep whipping until stiff peaks form. To the chocolate mixture, apply 1/4 of the cream and blend thoroughly. Then fold the remaining cream into this. Pour this chocolate mousse onto the cake and refrigerate until you get it finished.

Third Layer (Custard)

Beat egg yolks till they are light. Stir in sugar, flour, and gelatin and beat until combined. Bring it to a boil with cream and vanilla extract. Add a small amount of cream while adding to the egg mixture. Gradually add until all the cream is applied, and then pour the whole mixture into the pan through a strainer. Continue cooking before custard starts thickening. Cool slightly, then pour over the layer of chocolate mousse and freeze while the fourth layer is ready.

Fourth Layer (The Icing)

Please note this will make a lot of frosting, so don't worry about half this part of the recipe. Bring butter and cream to a boil, sprinkle with chocolate and let sit for five minutes. Disable to smooth. Let it cool before thickening begins. Take the cake from the oven, remove the pan collar from the cheesecake, then pour in some of the icings and use a spatula to spread it uniformly across the cake's top and sides. Place chocolate chips onto the side of the cake while this is still warm. Optional: melt half a cup (in the microwave) of white chocolate chips and swirl into the icing.

Let the cake refrigerate and then serve!

Nutrition: Calories 753.1 Cal, Fat 11 g, Carbs 113 g, Fiber 8 g, Sugar 84.8 g, Protein 11.2g

22.   *Soft Pretzel Bites (Auntie Anne's)*

Preparation time: 15 minutes
Cooking time: 12 minutes per batch
Servings: 20

Ingredients:

For regular pretzel bites

- 4 cups shredded, low moisture, part-skim mozzarella cheese
- 4 eggs, divided
- 2 tablespoons yeast
- 2 tablespoons baking powder
- 2 ounces cream cheese
- 3 cups almond flour
- 4 tablespoons low carb sweetener of your choice like swerve, erythritol, etc.
- Pretzel salt to sprinkle

For garlic herb pretzels: Optional

- 1 teaspoon minced thyme
- 2 cloves garlic, minced
- Freshly ground pepper to taste
- 1 teaspoon minced parsley
- For cinnamon pretzels: Optional
- ½ tablespoon ground cinnamon
- 4 tablespoons erythritol
- 1 ½ tablespoons butter, melted

For chocolate sauce: Optional

- 2.5 ounces stevia-sweetened chocolate, finely chopped
- 1/3 cup heavy cream
- For cheese sauce: Optional

- 6 tablespoons milk mixed with 1 teaspoon arrowroot powder
- 6 tablespoons freshly grated cheddar cheese
- Salt and pepper taste

Directions:

Line a baking sheet with parchment paper.

Place cream cheese and mozzarella cheese in a microwave-safe bowl and cook on high for about 1 ½ - 2 minutes or until melted and smooth. Stir every 30 seconds.

Add 2 eggs, yeast, baking powder, almond flour and sweetener and mix with an electric hand mixer until well incorporated.

Make 8 equal-sized balls and then shape it into a one-inch thick long rope.

Cut the rope into small parts, of about 1: 1 ½ inch size, using a pizza cutter.

Place it on the baking sheet. Leave a sufficient gap between the pretzel bites. If they don't fit on one sheet, use another baking sheet.

Beat the other 2 eggs lightly. Brush the egg on top of the pretzel bites. Sprinkle pretzel salt over it.

Bake in a preheated oven at 350° F for about 10: 12 minutes or until it becomes golden brown.

Cool for a few minutes before serving.

For garlic pretzels: use all ingredients for garlic herb pretzels and follow instructions from step 3 to step 1You can pair these with cheese sauce.

For cinnamon sugar pretzels: use all ingredients for cinnamon sugar pretzels and follow instructions from step 3 until step 10, but do not sprinkle pretzel salt while baking. You can pair these with chocolate sauce.

For chocolate sauce: add the chocolate into a heatproof bowl. Heat a saucepan with heavy cream on low heat. Once the cream starts to simmer, take it off the heat. In another bowl, add chocolate and the heavy cream. The chocolate will start melting with the heat of the cream. Whisk it well and your chocolate sauce is ready.

For cheese sauce: add arrowroot mixture into a small pan and heat it over a medium flame. Make sure you stir until the sauce becomes thick. Once you get the desired consistency, take it off heat.

Add cheese, salt and pepper and whisk well. Serve warm cheese sauce with garlic herb pretzels.

Tip: Serve pretzels with frozen lemonade.

Nutrition: 5 regular pretzels (not for garlic or cinnamon pretzels or cheese or chocolate sauce)
Calories 188 kcal, Fat 15 g, Total Carbohydrate 5 g, Net Carbohydrate 3 g, Fiber 2 g, Protein 11 g

23.   *Keto Bars (Kind)*

Preparation time: 5 minutes
Cooking time: 5 minutes
Servings: 6

Ingredients:
- 1 cup roasted, chopped almonds
- 3 tablespoons unsweetened coconut flakes
- 2 tablespoons clear fiber syrup
- 2 tablespoons powdered erythritol
- ¼ teaspoon sea salt
- ¼ cup roasted pumpkin seeds
- 1 tablespoon hemp seeds
- 2 tablespoons almond butter
- 1 teaspoon vanilla extract
- 1 medium vanilla bean, scraped

Directions:

Take a 6-inch square baking pan and line it with parchment paper.

Add almonds, coconut flakes, pumpkin seeds and hemp seeds to a bowl and stir.

Add fiber syrup, erythritol, almond butter and sea salt into a saucepan. Place the saucepan over medium flame. Stir frequently. When the mixture is smooth and well combined, turn off the heat.

Add vanilla bean and the extract. Pour into the bowl of almonds and mix well.

Spoon the mixture into the prepared baking dish. Spread it evenly.

Cool for 30 minutes in the baking dish itself.

Take out the parchment paper and the nut mixture and place on a cooling rack.

Cut into 6 equal bars and serve.

Store leftovers in an airtight container.

Tip: Do not add salt if the almonds or pumpkin seeds are salted.

Nutrition: 1 bar

Calories 216 kcal, Fat 18 g, Total Carbohydrate 7 g, Net Carbohydrate 3 g, Fiber 3 g, Protein 4 g

24. *Low Carb Banana Bread (Starbucks)*

Preparation time: 10 minutes
Cooking time: 60 minutes
Servings: 6

Ingredients:

For dry ingredients

- 2 tablespoons coconut flour
- 1 cup blanched almond flour
- ¼ cup chopped walnuts
- 1 teaspoon ground cinnamon
- 1 teaspoon baking powder
- 1/8 teaspoon salt (optional)
- ¼ teaspoon xanthan gum (optional)

For wet ingredients

- ¼ cup allulose
- 2 large eggs
- 1 teaspoon banana extract
- 2 tablespoons unsweetened almond milk
- 3 tablespoons butter

Directions:

Line a small loaf pan (8 x 4 inches) with a large sheet of parchment paper so that it overhangs from it (on the width sides).

Add all the dry ingredients into a bowl and stir well.

Add allulose and butter to a bowl and mix with an electric mixer until creamy.

Add eggs and beat on low speed until well combined. Beat in the almond milk and banana extract.

Mix the dry ingredients with the wet ingredients. Continue beating on low speed until smooth and free from lumps.

Add walnuts and stir.

Spoon the batter into the prepared loaf pan.

Bake in a preheated oven at 350° F for about 5 minutes or until brown on top.

Let the bread cool in the pan completely. Lift the bread along with the parchment paper and carefully peel off the paper.

Cut into 6 equal slices and serve. You should get slices of about 1 ¾ inch thick. The nutritional value mentioned is of this size.

Tip: You can sprinkle some extra walnuts on top (step 7). Xanthan gum is recommended because the bread tends to crumble. It is better if you wait 18-24 hours before slicing the bread.

Nutrition: Calories 224 kcal, Fat 20 g, Total Carbohydrate 6 g, Net Carbohydrate 2 g, Fiber 4 g, Protein 8 g

25. *Cranberry Bliss Bars (Starbucks)*

<u>Preparation time:</u> 10 minutes
<u>Cooking time:</u> 25 minutes
<u>Servings</u>: 8

Ingredients:

- 3 tablespoons butter, cubed, softened
- ½ teaspoon molasses (optional, only for flavor)
- 1 egg, at room temperature
- ¼ teaspoon orange extract
- 2 tablespoons coconut flour
- 2 tablespoons almond flour
- 2 tablespoons golden ground flax seeds
- 1/8 teaspoon ground ginger (optional)
- A tiny pinch salt
- 3 tablespoons erythritol or xylitol
- ½ cup finely chopped fresh cranberries
- ½ teaspoon vanilla extract

- ½ teaspoon baking powder
- A pinch ground cinnamon (optional)
- ¼ teaspoon stevia powder

For frosting

- 2 ounces cream cheese, softened
- 2 drops lemon extract
- ½ teaspoon grated orange zest (optional)
- ¼ cup powdered xylitol or erythritol
- ½ tablespoon butter

Directions:

Place butter and sweetener in a bowl, mix with an electric hand mixer until creamy.

Add egg, continue beating, then add vanilla, molasses, and orange extracts.

Mix all dry ingredients in another bowl and then combine them with the wet ingredients.

Grease a 6-inch pan with cooking spray. Pour the batter into the pan.

Bake in a preheated oven at 350° F for about 18 to 22 minutes. Ensure that you do not over bake it.

Remove the pan from the oven and place on a wire rack to cool completely.

Mix together fresh cranberries and stevia in a bowl.

To make frosting: add cream cheese, orange zest, sweetener, lemon extract and butter in a mixing bowl. Beat until creamy with an electric mixer.

Spoon the frosting over the baked bars. Scatter cranberries on top.

Cut into 8 equal triangles and serve.

Transfer leftovers in an airtight container and refrigerate until further use.

Tip: You can add some dried cranberries to the batter before baking.

Nutrition: Calories 110 kcal, Fat 10 g, Total Carbohydrate 3 g, Net Carbohydrate 2 g, Fiber 1 g, Protein 2 g

26.   *Cheddar Bay Biscuits (Red Lobster)*

Preparation time: 15 minutes
Cooking time: 10 minutes
Servings: 18

Ingredients:
- 3 cups superfine almond flour
- 2 tablespoons baking powder
- 4 large eggs
- 8 tablespoons unsalted butter, melted
- 1 cup sour cream
- 2 teaspoons garlic powder
- ½ teaspoon salt
- 1 cup grated cheddar cheese
- For garlic butter topping:
- 4 tablespoons butter, melted
- 2 tablespoons minced parsley
- 1 teaspoon garlic powder

Directions:
Grease 3 muffin pans of 6 counts each with some cooking spray.

Add almond flour, garlic powder and baking powder into a bowl and mix well

Stir together sour cream, eggs and butter in a bowl. Pour this mixture into the bowl of dry ingredients. Stir until you get sticky dough.

Add cheese and stir.

Divide the batter into the muffin pans.

Bake in a preheated oven at 450° F for about 12 minutes or until golden.

Remove the muffin pans from the oven and allow it to cool for a few minutes. Run a knife around the edges to loosen the biscuits.

To make garlic butter topping: add butter, garlic powder and parsley into a small bowl and mix well.

Take the baking sheet out of the oven. Brush the biscuits with butter mixture and allow them to cool for a few minutes.

Serve.

Tip: You can replace parsley with oregano in the garlic butter topping. It will give altogether a different flavor.

Nutrition: Calories 240 kcal, Fat 22 g, Total Carbohydrate 5 g, Net Carbohydrate 3 g, Fiber 2 g, Protein 7 g

27.   *Olive Garden Roasted Butternut Squash*

<u>Preparation Time:</u> 10 minutes

<u>Cooking Time:</u> 1 hour

<u>Servings:</u> 6

Ingredients:

- Butternut squash - 8 cups
- Salt - 1 teaspoon
- Sweet white wine - 1 cup (Riesling works well)
- Vegetable oil - 2 tablespoons

Directions:

Heat your oven to 400 degrees F. Spray a 9-by13-inch baking dish with cooking spray.

Toss the butternut squash, salt and oil in a bowl. Spread the mixture on a rimmed baking sheet and place in the oven to bake for approx. 30 minutes. Move the squash pieces to the prepared baking dish, pour the wine over the squash, then place in the oven to bake for about 20 more minutes, until the squash is tender. Smaller squash pieces will take a shorter time to cook. Serve immediately.

Nutrition:

Calories 157 Cal, Fat 4 g, Carbs 22 g, Fiber 3 g, Sugar 4 g, Protein 1 g, Calories 154 kcal, Cholesterol 0mg, Calcium 93mg, Saturated Fat 3g, Potassium 685mg, Sodium 397mg, Vitamin C 39.2mg, Vitamin A 19845IU, Iron: 1.4mg

28.   *Bonefish Grill's Cloud Sugar Pie Bar*

Preparation Time: 10 minutes
Cooking Time: 1 hour
Servings: 12

Ingredients:
- Twenty four graham crackers smashed
- Unsalted butter of 12 teaspoons, melted
- 5 oz of an instant mix of vanilla pudding (145 g)
- 2 1/2 cups of (600 mL) heavy cream
- 1/2 cup (85 g) chocolate candy pieces
- Whipped cream, to be served

Directions:
Line the parchment paper with a baking sheet.

Mix the graham cracker crumbs and butter in a medium bowl until thoroughly integrated.

Pour the crumbs onto the baking sheet that has been prepared and push tightly into an even plate. Transfer to the refrigerator for 1 hour, roughly.

Combine the pudding mix and heavy cream in the bowl of a stand mixer fitted with the whisk attachment, and whip until light and fluffy, for around 5 minutes.

Spread the pudding and cover with the candy bits over the crust.

Cut into 12 bars with a dollop of whipped cream and serve.

Nutrition: Per Serving:

Calories 291 kcal, Protein 4.4g, Carbohydrates 45.7g, Fat 10.7g, Cholesterol 92.6mg, Sodium 88.1mg

29. *Maggiano's Little Italy's CHOCO COOKIES CHIP*

Preparation Time: 10 minutes

Cooking Time: 10 minutes

Servings: 15

Ingredients:

- 1 cup of brown sugar
- 1 cup of sugar caster
- 1 Amul butter stick
- Two chickens
- 2 teaspoons of an extract of vanilla
- 1 teaspoon powder for baking
- 1/4 teaspoon of salt
- 3 cups of flour Maida
- 1 dark chocolate chip cup
- Butter to grease the pan

Directions:

Combine the brown sugar and caster sugar.

Let the butter melt. When paired with the sugars, ensure it is at room temperature.

One at a time, add the eggs. Mix thoroughly.

Add the essence of vanilla, baking powder, and salt.

In batches, incorporate the Maida.

Add the chocolate chips now.

Mix well for all the ingredients.

Oven for 10 minutes, preheat at 300 ° F (150 ° C).

In the meantime, by adding butter, prepare the baking pan.

Break the dough into small balls, leaving 1½-2 inch holes between the dough.

For 15-17 minutes, bake.

Take the tray out until the timer goes off and let the cookies cool on it; they could get trapped in the tray.

Nutrition: Per Serving:

Calories 125 kcal, Protein 1.5g, Carbohydrates 15.5g, Fat 7.1g, Cholesterol 17.9mg, Sodium 63.1mg

30.   Shake Shack's *LIGHT SWEET CAKE OF POTATO*

Preparation Time: 10 minutes
Cooking Time: 1 hour
Servings: 8

Ingredients:

- 1 1/2 cups flour (185 g)
- 1/2 cup of wheat flour (65 g)
- 2 bread powder teaspoons
- 1/2 teaspoon of baking soda
- 1 cinnamon teaspoon
- 1/8 teaspoon of salt
- 1/4 teaspoon of ginger
- Two chickens
- 1/2 teaspoon vanilla vanilla
- 1/2 cup (120 mL) milk
- 1/4 cup (60 mL) oil
- 2/3 cup sugar (135 g)
- 2 tablespoons of honey
- 1 cup (260 g) of sweet potato purée
- For serving, peanut butter (optional)

Directions:

Then, combine the dry ingredients separately with the wet ingredients.

Mix them then.

Pour into a pan of the loaf

Bake for 50 minutes to 1 hour at 350 ° F (180 ° C) in the oven.

Optional: with peanut butter, serve it.

Nutrition:

Calories 291, Protein 4.4g, Carbohydrates 45.7g, Fat 10.7g, Cholesterol 92.6mg, Sodium 88.1mg

31. Ci Ci's Cherry Dessert Pizza

Preparation Time: 40-45 minutes
Cooking Time: 15 minutes
Servings: 8

Ingredients:

The Pizza

- Cherry pie filling (20 oz. can)
- Pizza mix (1 pkg.)
- Crumb topping (.25 cup)

The Topping

- Brown sugar (1 tbsp.)
- Flour (.5 cup)
- Sugar (3 tbsp.)
- Softened butter (.25 cup)
- Salt (1/8 tsp.)

Directions:

Warm the oven to reach 450° Fahrenheit. Lightly spritz a pizza pan with cooking oil spray.

Prepare the pizza dough per the package instructions and spread it onto the prepared pan. Prick it with a fork eight to ten times. Place the pan in the hot oven to bake for five minutes.

Transfer the cooked crust from the oven and add the pie filling over the hot crust. Sprinkle it with ¼ of a cup of crumb topping and bake for another 20 to 25 minutes. Remove the pizza when the dough is golden brown.

Prepare the topping. Whisk the dry fixings (flour, sugar, brown sugar, and salt). Combine all of the components until the topping resembles cornmeal.

32.   *Ci Ci's Chocolate Dessert Pizza*

<u>Preparation Time:</u> 35 minutes

<u>Cooking Time:</u> 15 minutes

<u>Servings</u>: 8

Ingredients:

The Pizza

- Pizza dough mix (1 pkg.)
- Chocolate pudding mix - cooked & cooled (3.4 oz. box)

The Mix

- Sugar (3 tbsp.)
- Flour (.5 cup)
- Salt (1/8 tsp.)
- Brown sugar (1 tbsp.)
- Softened butter (.25 cup)

Note: The pudding mix should be the cooked type - not instant.

Directions:

Warm the oven at 450° Fahrenheit.

Prepare the pizza dough per the package instructions.

Stretch and shape the dough on a greased pizza pan. Pierce the dough with a fork eight to ten times. Bake for about five minutes.

Remove the pan from the oven and spread ¾ of a cup of chocolate pudding over the dough and sprinkle with ¼ of a cup of the crumb topping. Pop it back in the oven and bake until it's crispy (18-20 min.).

Mix the flour, sugar, salt, and brown sugar. Blend in the butter until it resembles cornmeal.

33. *Godfather's Pizza: Cinnamon Streusel Dessert Pizza*

Preparation Time: 25 minutes

Cooking Time: 10 minutes

Servings: 3-4 or 8 slices

Ingredients:

- Pizza dough (homemade or store-bought)
- Melted butter (1 tbsp.)
- Cinnamon

The Streusel

- A-P flour (1/2 cup + 1/3 cup)
- White sugar (1/3 cup)
- Olive oil (2 tbsp.)
- Vegetable shortening (2 tbsp.)
- Brown sugar (.25 cup)

The Icing

- Powdered sugar (1 cup)
- Milk (1 tbsp.)
- Vanilla (.5 tsp.)
- Also Needed: 12-inch pizza pan

Directions:

Whisk the streusel ingredients and set side aside. Lightly spritz the pizza pan using a cooking oil spray.

Pat the dough into the pan. "Poke" the dough with a fork to reduce air bubbles while baking. Melt one tablespoon of butter and brush the dough. Sprinkle cinnamon all around the buttered crust. Top the pizza crust with the streusel mix.

Bake at 460° Fahrenheit for eight to nine minutes.

Combine the icing fixings until it has a drizzle consistency.

Decorate the pie using the icing in a circular pinwheel pattern. Slice and serve.

DRINKS

34. Olive Garden Pomegranate Margarita Martini

Preparation Time: 5 minutes
Cooking Time: 0
Servings: 1

Ingredients:

- 2 ounces of sweet-and-sour mix
- 2 teaspoons of orange juice
- 1 teaspoon of lime juice
- 1 ½ ounces of real grenadine syrup
- ¾ ounce of Patron Citronge Orange Liqueur
- 1 ounce of Patron Silver Tequila

Garnish

- Thin lime slice
- Thin lemon slice

Directions:

Put a handful of ice into a shaker and then pour the liquids in it.

Shake well.

Chill a 10-ounce martini glass, then pour the entire drink from the shaker into the glass.

Drop the lemon and lime slice to float on the surface of the drink, then enjoy!

Tip: Make sure you shake the drink well to get it fully mixed.

Nutrition: Calories 218 Cal, Fat 0.21 g, Carbs 52.06 g, Fiber 0.1 g, Sugar 47.48 g, Protein 0.38 g

35.   *Olive Garden Mango Martini*

<u>Preparation Time</u>: 10 minutes
<u>Cooking Time</u>: 0 minutes
<u>Servings</u>: 1

Ingredients:
- 2 ounces of sweet-and-sour mix
- 2 ounces of mango nectar
- ¾ ounce of triple sec
- 2 ounces of Malibu Mango rum

Garnish
- A lime slice

Directions:

Put a handful of ice into a shaker. Add all the ingredients into it, then shake well.

Chill a 10-ounce martini glass, then pour the drink from the shaker into it.

Add a slice of lime to the rim of the glass and serve.

Tip: Chilling the glass beforehand keeps the drink colder longer.

Nutrition: Calories 180 Cal, Fat 4.3 g, Carbs 33.62 g, Fiber 1.4 g, Sugar 28.05 g, Protein: 4.13 g

36.   *Olive Garden Limoncello Lemonade*

Preparation Time: 8 minutes

Cooking Time: 0 minutes

Servings: 1

Ingredients:

- 2 cups of ice
- 4 ounces of lemonade
- 1 ounce of limoncello liqueur
- 1 ounce of Smirnoff Citrus Vodka
- 4 teaspoons of lemon juice
- ¼ cup of granulated sugar (you can try brown sugar if you wish)
- ¼ cup of hot water

Garnish

- 1 slice of lemon

Directions:

Prepare a lemon syrup by mixing lemon juice, sugar, and hot water.

Let the syrup chill.

Prepare the drink by mixing ¾ ounce of chilled lemon syrup with limoncello, citrus vodka, lemonade, and ice. You will need to put them all in a blender on high speed. Blend until the ice is crushed (but don't put all the ice in at once, just one cube at a time) since you are trying to make the drink slushy.

Chill a 16-ounce martini glass, then pour in the drink from the blender. Decorate the glass with a lemon slice on the rim of the glass, and enjoy.

Tip: I recommend Country Time or Minute Maid lemonade.

Nutrition: Calories 822 Cal, Fat 33.87 g, Carbs 112.7 g, Fiber 12.9 g, Sugar: 63.91 g, Protein 8.73 g

37. *Starbucks Pink Drink*

Preparation time: 5 minutes
Cooking time: 0 minutes
Serving: 2

Ingredients:
- 2 cups passion tea, brewed, cooled
- ½ cup heavy cream
- 2 tablespoons vanilla syrup, sugar-free
- 1 ½ cup ice cubes

Directions
Add all the ingredients in the order into a food processor except for ice, shut with the lid, and then pulse for 1 minute until smooth.

Divide the ice cubes evenly between two glasses, pour in the drink, and then serve.

Nutrition: 379 Cal; 21 g Fats; 2 g Protein; 4 g Net Carb; 0 g Fiber;

38.   *Starbucks Iced Matcha Latte*

Preparation time: 5 minutes
Cooking time: 0 minutes
Serving: 2

Ingredients:

- 2 cups almond milk, unsweetened
- 2 tablespoons vanilla syrup, sugar-free
- 2 tablespoons avocado oil
- 2 teaspoons matcha powder
- 2 cups of ice cubes

Directions

Add all the ingredients in the order into a food processor except for ice, shut with the lid, and then pulse for 1 minute until smooth.

Divide the ice cubes evenly between two glasses, pour in the latte, and then serve.

Nutrition: 199 Cal; 16.1 g Fats; 5 g Protein; 4 g Net Carb; 4.5 g Fiber;

Preparation time: 5 minutes

Cooking time: 0 minutes

Serving: 2

Ingredients:

- ½ cup heavy cream
- ½ cup strong coffee, brewed, cooled
- ¾ tablespoons erythritol sweetener
- 3 tablespoons caramel sauce, low-carb
- 1 ½ cups ice cubes
- 1/4 cup whipping cream

Directions

Add all the ingredients in the order into a food processor except for whipping cream, shut with the lid, and then pulse for 1 minute until smooth.

Divide the drink evenly between two glasses, top with the whipped cream, and then serve.

Nutrition: 182 Cal; 14.7 g Fats; 1 g Protein; 0.5 g Net Carb; 0.6 g Fiber;

40.   *Starbucks Pumpkin Spice Frappuccino*

Preparation time: 5 minutes
Cooking time: 0 minutes
Serving: 2

Ingredients:
- 2/3 cup almond milk, vanilla flavored, unsweetened
- 2/3 cup pumpkin puree
- 2/3 cup coconut milk, unsweetened
- 1 ½ teaspoon pumpkin pie spice and more for topping
- 1 teaspoon vanilla extract, unsweetened
- 2 teaspoons liquid stevia
- 4 teaspoons instant coffee granules
- 2 cups of ice cubes
- ½ cup whipped coconut cream

Directions:
Add all the ingredients in the order into a food processor except for whipped cream, shut with the lid, and then pulse for 1 minute until smooth.

Divide the drink evenly between two glasses, top with the whipped cream, sprinkle with pumpkin pie spice, and then serve.

Nutrition: 263.5 Cal; 23.4 g Fats; 3.3 g Protein; 7.7 g Net Carb; 2.2 g Fiber;

41.Starbucks Peppermint Mocha Coffee

Preparation time: 5 minutes
Cooking time: 2 minutes
Serving: 2

Ingredients:

- 2 cups almond milk, unsweetened
- 1 cup brewed coffee, cooled
- 4 tablespoons heavy whipping cream
- ½ teaspoon peppermint extract, unsweetened
- 2 tablespoons cocoa powder
- 6 tablespoons Swerve Confectioners
- 2 tablespoons MCT Oil Powder, Chocolate flavored
- ½ cup whipped cream
- 2 teaspoons chocolate shavings, low carb

Directions

Add all the ingredients in the order into a food processor except for whipped cream, peppermint extract, and chocolate shavings, shut with the lid, and then pulse for 1 minute until smooth.

Pour the mixture into a medium pan, place it over medium heat and cook for 2 minutes until warm.

Remove the pan from heat, add peppermint extract and then stir until mixed.

Divide the drink evenly between two glasses, top with whipped cream, sprinkle with chocolate shavings, and then serve.

Nutrition: 197 Cal; 19 g Fats; 1 g Protein; 2.4 g Net Carb; 2.8 g Fiber;

42.   *Vanilla Bean Frappuccino*

Preparation time: 5 minutes
Cooking time: 0 minutes
Serving: 2

Ingredients:

- ½ cup heavy whipping cream
- 1 cups vanilla almond milk, unsweetened
- ½ teaspoon liquid stevia, vanilla flavored
- ½ of vanilla bean, split lengthwise, inside scraped out
- ½ cup whipped cream
- 1 cup of ice cubes
- 2 teaspoons chocolate shavings, low-carb

Directions:

Add all the ingredients in the order into a food processor except for whipped cream, ice, and chocolate shavings, shut with the lid, and then pulse for 1 minute until smooth.

Add ice and then continue blending for 30 seconds until the ice has crushed

Divide the drink evenly between two glasses, top with the whipped cream, sprinkle with chocolate shavings, and then serve.

Nutrition: 217 Cal; 23 g Fats; 1 g Protein; 2 g Net Carb; 0 g Fiber;

43. *Irish Cream Liqueur*

Preparation time: 5 minutes
Cooking time: 7 minutes
Serving: 12

Ingredients:

- 1 teaspoon vanilla extract, unsweetened
- 1 tablespoon cocoa powder
- 2/3 cup erythritol sweetener
- 1 teaspoon almond extract, unsweetened
- 1 teaspoon instant coffee
- 1 1/3 cups Irish whiskey
- 2 cups heavy cream

Directions:

Take a small saucepan, place it over medium heat, add cream and erythritol, whisk well and then cook for 3 minutes until sweetener has dissolved.

Then add coffee, cocoa powder, both extracts, whisk well until well combined and then remove the pan from heat.

Pour in whiskey, stir until well combined, pour the mixture into an air-tight jar, cover with the lid and let it chill in the refrigerator until ready to use.

Nutrition: 138 Cal; 14.1 g Fats; 1.4 g Protein; 1.5 g Net Carb; 0.3 g Fiber;

44.   *Chick-fil-A Frozen Lemonade*

Preparation time: 5 minutes
Cooking time: 0 minutes
Serving: 2

Ingredients:
1 packet lemonade mix, sugar-free
2 cups vanilla ice cream, sugar-free
¼ cup lemon juice
1 cup of water

Directions
Add all the ingredients in the order into a food processor except ice cream, shut with the lid, and then pulse for 10 seconds until smooth.
Add ice cream and then continue blending for 10 seconds until the drink reaches to desired consistency.
Divide the lemonade between two glasses and then serve.

Nutrition: 546 Cal; 45.5 g Fats; 5.5 g Protein; 28 g Net Carb; 5.5 g Fiber;

45.   *Starbucks White Drink*

Preparation time: 5 minutes
Cooking time: 0 minutes
Serving: 2

Ingredients

- 1 teaspoon vanilla extract, unsweetened
- 1 cup peach white tea, brewed
- ½ cup whipped coconut cream
- 2/3 cup coconut cream
- 1 cup of ice cubes

Directions

Add all the ingredients in the order into a food processor except whipped cream, shut with the lid, and then pulse for 30 seconds until smooth.

Divide the drink between two glasses, top evenly with whipped cream and then serve.

Nutrition: 168 Cal; 18 g Fats; 2 g Protein; 4 g Net Carb; 0 g Fiber;

46.   *Frappuccino At Starbucks*

Preparation time: 5 minutes
Cooking Time: 0 minutes
Servings: 6

Ingredients:

- 1 cup strong cooled coffee
- 1 cup heavy cream
- 1 ½ tbsp. stevia erythritol blend
- ⅓ cups of ice

Optional Garnish

- Whipped cream & additional low-carb caramel sauce

Directions:

Use an electric blender with ice crushing capacity, and combine each of the fixings. Blend until smooth - as a slushie.

Pour the mixture into chilled glasses and serve with whipped cream and low-carb caramel sauce to your liking.

Nutrition: Calories 182 kcal, Protein 1g, Carbs 1.2g, Fat 14.7g, Fiber 0.6g

47. *Iced Skinny Vanilla Latte & Frappuccino At Starbucks*

Preparation time: 5 minutes
Cooking Time: 0 minutes
Servings: 6

Ingredients:

The Concentrate

- 1 ½ cups almond milk
- ½ cup heavy cream
- 1 cup very very strong coffee (about double the regular amount of grounds)
- ½ cup - natural sweetener (below recipe)
- 1 tsp. vanilla

Directions:

Make the Concentrate: Toss all of the components and thoroughly mix them.

To Make an Iced Latte:

1 part concentrate = 1 to 1.5 parts almond milk + coffee ice cubes (frozen coffee in an ice cube tray)

Latte Example: 6 oz. concentrate + 8 oz. of almond milk over frozen coffee ice cubes

To Make a Frappuccino:

Blend 1 part concentrate, coffee ice cubes and regular ice cubes, a pinch of xanthan gum, and ½ part almond milk.

Frappuccino Example: 8 oz. concentrate + 4 oz. almond milk blended with 6 coffee ice cubes, 6 regular ice cubes, and a pinch of xanthan gum.

Nutrition: Calories 79 kcal, Protein 0g, Carbs 0g, Fat 8g, Fiber 0g

48. Natural Keto-Friendly Sugar Sweetener

Preparation time: 5 minutes
Cooking Time: 0 minutes
Servings: 64 tablespoons

Ingredients:
- 12 oz. or 1 ½ cups + 2 tbsp. erythritol
- 16 oz. or 2 cups + 2 tbsp. xylitol
- 2 tsp. pure stevia extract

Directions:
Granular Sweetener: For baking and candy making, you can just mix the ingredients together by hand.

Powdered Sweetener: Process the ingredients in the food processor for a few minutes if you are planning on using it in chocolate, beverages, or icing.

Nutrition: Calories 1, Carbs 0.1g, Fiber 0.1g

49.   *Orange Julius by Dairy Queen*

Preparation time: 5 minutes
Cooking Time: 0 minutes
Servings: 2

Ingredients:

- 2/3 cup heavy whipping cream
- 3 tbsp./as desired of confectioners erythritol
- 2 to 3 oz. cream cheese
- 1 ½ tsp. pure orange extract
- 1 ½ tsp. lemon juice
- 2 to 2 ½ cups crushed ice

Optional Ingredients

- Food coloring

To Garnish

- Orange slice

Directions:

Add heavy whipping cream to a blender. Blend for a minute or so until the cream has churned into a thick whipped cream.

Add the cream cheese, erythritol, pure orange extract, lemon juice, food coloring , and crushed ice. Using crushed ice vs. ice cubes helps the shake come together quickly. Blend until even and smooth, about a minute.

Pour into one large or two small glasses. Garnish with an orange slice if desired.

Notes: Dairy Queen bought the Orange Julius chain in 1987 and began adding it to its small Treat Center locations the following year.

Nutrition: Calories 367 kcal, Protein 2g, Carbs 15.5g, Fat 42g, Fiber 0g

50.   *Peppermint Mocha at Starbucks*

Preparation time: 3 minutes
Cooking Time: 0 minutes
Servings: 1

Ingredients:

- 2 tbsp. heavy whipping cream
- 1 cup unsweetened (carton only) coconut/almond milk
- 4 oz. brewed blonde roast coffee
- 1 tbsp. Dutch-process cocoa powder
- 3 tbsp. Swerve Confectioners
- 1 tbsp. Perfect Keto Chocolate MCT Oil Powder
- ¼ tsp. or as desired - peppermint extract
- 100% cacao chocolate or another keto-friendly chocolate shavings

Optional: Keto-friendly whipped cream

Directions:

Combine all of the fixings (omit the peppermint extract) using an electric whisk to make the process much simpler. Place them in a pan to warm using the medium-temperature setting.

Warm the mixture to your desired temperature (2 min.), turn off the heat, add the peppermint extract, and mix it again.

Pour the treat into a glass, top it off using your favorite keto-friendly whipped cream and/or chocolate shavings to serve.

Nutrition: Calories: 197, Protein: 1g, Carbs: 5.2g, Fat: 19g, Fiber: 2.8g

51. Shamrock Shake From McDonald's

Preparation time: 6 minutes

Cooking Time: 0 minutes

Servings: 2 glasses

Ingredients:

- 2 cups of ice cream (vanilla)
- 10 drops of food coloring (green)
- Whipped cream and cherries
- ¾ cup of whole milk
- ¼ tsp. of mint extract

Directions:

Switch on the blender and place the milk, mint extract, food coloring, and ice cream in it.

Blend the ingredients until they become smooth.

Pour them in the tall glasses (two) and crown each of them with cream, cherries, and sprinkles to serve.

Nutrition: Calories 330 kcal, Carb 15g, Protein 7g, Fat 17g, Fiber 0g

52.   *Wendy's Inspired Keto Chocolate Frosty*

Preparation time: 10 minutes
Cooking Time: 0 minutes
Servings: 4

Ingredients:
- 1 cup heavy whipping cream
- 1 tbsp. almond butter
- 2 tbsp. unsweetened cocoa powder
- 5-10 drops - to taste of Stevia
- 1 tsp. vanilla extract

Directions:
Combine all of the fixings using an electric mixer until it forms stiff peaks.

Pop the mixture into the freezer for 30 minutes to one hour or until it's barely frozen.

Dump the 'frosty' mixture into a plastic freezer bag.

Make a piping bag by snipping the corner from the bag. Pipe the frosty into the chilled glasses.

Nutrition: Calories 241 kcal, Protein 3g, Carbs 4g, Fat 25 g, Fiber 1g

CONCLUSION

I hope you are geared for your new dining experience after reading each chapter of Copycat Recipes.

If you have any concerns about alcohol, put them to rest. Alcohol will start to evaporate at three times the rate of water when combined. You can speed the process by leaving the lid off the skillet/pan. (An open cover will lead to faster evaporation compared to a closed top.)

However, you will need to cook food for about three hours to erase all traces of alcohol. After an hour of cooking, 25% of the alcohol remains, and even after two and a half hours, there's still 5% of it.

The Italians figured it out; alcohol is versatile! Whether you use a rum, sake, or beer, alcohol is a perfect flavor enhancer, tenderizer, as a marinade, or simmered in sauces. Italians love it! The next step is to decide which dish you want to prepare first. That is the significant part; you have the recipes for a ton of restaurant-style menu items to choose from for your family and friends to enjoy!